Bride's · Little · Book · of

CAKES
and
TOASTS

CLARKSON N. POTTER / PUBLISHERS, NEW YORK

acknowledgments

BRIDE'S especially wants to thank DONNA FERRARI, Tabletop, Food & Wine Editor, whose ideas and vision have inspired wedding-cake bakers and photographers to new levels of creativity. BRIDE'S also thanks ANDREA FELD, Managing Editor, for her invaluable contribution to the romance and style of the text, and for keeping the project on track. A hearty toast of gratitude to ROCHELLE UDELL of The Condé Nast Publications — for making this book happen — to LAUREN SHAKELY of Clarkson N. Potter, and to BRIDE'S Art Director PHYLLIS RICHMOND COX. Thanks to Kathy Mullins, the book's writer/researcher. And appreciation to BRIDE'S staff members Wendy Caisse Curran, Ashley Thompson, and Wendy Marder, for handling copy editing, photographers' permissions, and fact checking, respectively. And, a very special thank you to all the talented cake artists and professionals whose work appears in this book.

Bakers : Ellen Baumwoll, Bijoux Doux Specialty Cakes & Pastries, N.Y.C. (pg.15, 28-29); Margaret Braun, N.Y.C. (pg. 17); Cile Bellefleur Burbidge, Danvers, MA (pg. 13); Cheryl Kleinman, N.Y.C. (cover; pg. 18; 21, bottom; 33); Lisa Montenegro, Cakeability, N.Y.C. (page 10); Lisa Montenegro and Georgia Kavanaugh (title pg.; pg. 11); Patti Paige, Baked Ideas, N.Y.C. (pg. 37); Patisserie Lanciani, N.Y.C. (pg. 4); Kevin Pavlina, Northville, MI (pg. 12, 14, 25); Colette Peters, Colette's Cakes, N.Y.C. (pg. 6, 8); Betty Van Norstrand, Poughkeepsie, NY (pg. 20, top; 24); Gail Watson, N.Y.C. (pg. 20, bottom; pg. 21, top); Sylvia Weinstock, N.Y.C. (pg. 16, 26-27); Scott Woolley, Michael Farace, N.Y.C. (pg. 19).

Photographers : Tohru Nakamura (pg. 3); Peter Bosch (pg. 30-31); Antoine Bootz (pg.36); Todd Eberle (cover; pg. 17; 21, bottom; 22-23; 33); Rita Maas (pg. 4, 37); Michael Mundy (pg. 10, 26-27); Carin & David Riley (pg. 13, 18, 19, 25); Maria Robledo (title page, pg. 6, 14, 40); Karl Stoecker (pg. 20, bottom); William Waldron (pg. 8; 11; 16; 21, top; 28-29); Lisa Charles Watson (pg. 12, 15, 20, top); Henry Wolf (pg. 24).

Additional Credits : "Faneuil" monogrammed sterling silver cake knife, Tiffany & Co., (pg. 22); Floral designs: Bill Crinnigan, N.Y.C. (pg. 28-29); Paul Bott, Twigs, N.Y.C. (pg. 30-31); Napkin, A2 (pg. 36); Punch recipe courtesy of Moët & Chandon Champagne; Cake recipe courtesy of Kevin Pavlina.

Published by Clarkson N. Potter, 201 East 50th Street, New York, New York 10022. Member of the Crown Publishing Group. CLARKSON N. POTTER, POTTER, and colophon are trademarks of Clarkson N. Potter. Manufactured in Hong Kong.

Design by Justine Strasberg

Library of Congress Cataloging–in–Publication Data
Bride's little book of cakes and toasts / by the editors of Bride's magazine
1. Wedding cakes. 2. Wedding toasts. I. Brides (The Condé Nast Publications Inc.)
TX771. B84 1993p.   92-23017
641 . 8'653 — dc20   CIP
ISBN 0-517-59296-7
10 9 8 7 6 5 4 3 2 1   First Edition

contents

Savor the moments: the vows, the kiss, the first dance, and then...the CAKE. Amid the excitement of celebration and feasting, all eyes and hearts focus upon the bride and groom as they slice—with beribboned knife or sword—the tiers of joy and sculpted icing that are symbolic of their love. The wedding cakes that have been collected for this treasury are contemporary works of art that taste as delicious as they look. Each makes a personal statement about the couple them-

introduction

selves.... Then the toasts begin—some halting but so sincere they bring tears to the eyes, others admirably eloquent and polished tributes, a few downright funny but in good taste. Once the province of "men only," toasts are now shared by all members of the family. These annealing words, this mortar that cements families together, cast a spell that no photograph can capture. Truly, a toast pleases all the senses: taste, smell, touch, sight, and...(clink) hearing. Now, here's "Health, love, and money—and time to enjoy them...."

BARBARA TOBER

Editor-in-Chief, BRIDE'S magazine

Trompe l'oeil packages made of cake: a delectable flavor surprise.

The wedding cake is the pièce de résistance of the wedding reception, a personal expression of a couple's tastes, heritages, wedding theme. Imagine layers of pound cake; cheesecake; fruitcake; lemon cake; cherry cake; carrot cake or spice cake; nut torte; chocolate, banana-nut, mocha, or hazelnut cake...iced in chocolate, white chocolate or delicate buttercream, gold or silver filigree...filled with raspberry, praline, apricot, and chocolate mousse, laced with a liqueur (perhaps Grand Marnier or a sweet framboise). Layers may be curved like rounded domes, stacked, supported

cake style, flavor, personality

in tiers, or shaped like a heart, rectangle, or square—even a tennis racquet, guitar, book, top hat, sports car—to evoke a leisure-time interest. The icing on the country-style cake (left) is "quilted" (an activity symbolizing community friendship) with quaint symbols: a pair of doves promising marital harmony, and, in pastillage (or gum/sugar paste), hearts symbolizing fidelity; sunbursts, stars, a floral topper.

A cake decorated with symbols of marital happiness.

The wedding cake, once called bride cake, and later bride's cake, was initially a symbol of bounty and good luck. The cake, left, with its topper of spun-sugar sheaves of wheat, evokes the harvest—a time when Roman brides carried wheat sheaves to ensure their future fertility. Over the years, it became customary for the wheat to be baked with salt into a simple hard biscuit used during Roman Empire wedding ceremonies. Together, the bride and groom sealed their mar-

cake lore

riage by eating crumbs from this biscuit. The remainder was crumbled over the bride's head by the wedding officiant—as a wish for plenty, good fortune, many children; guests rushed forward to claim a lucky fragment. This has evolved into today's tradition that all wedding guests sample (or take home) a piece of wedding cake for good luck. The succulent marzipan grapes on the cake, right, pay tribute to Bacchus, the Greek god of wine and celebration, and also forecast bounty, fruitfulness, happiness, and good cheer.

Symbols of bounty — wheat sheaves [ABOVE], *grapes* [RIGHT].

Pièce montée: handmolded flowers, filigree, delicate stringwork.

Architectural influence: a Victorian love of gazebos, terraces.

Victorian cakes of the late nineteenth century were edible valentines—romantic confections festooned with sentimental hearts, oversized cabbage roses, brightly hued pansies, vibrant peonies, and love tokens. With their characteristic decorative excess, the Victorians created fanciful tiers: icing emulated lace and latticework; spun-sugar ivy, violets,

A cake shaped like a fan — a symbol of Victorian courtship.

and lilacs clung to trellised vines. Victorian sweets—cakes were no exception—were often infused with rosewater, rose syrup, and rose petals, then garnished with crystallized rose petals. The fan cake, left, is reminiscent of the fondant cakes of Victorian times; fans were traditional courtship gifts, easily personalized with love inscriptions, secret messages, and flowers. The Victorian-style cake, right, has a delicate lacework design interwoven with ribbon and the rounded tiers common in Australian work; cabbage roses, cupids, swags, trellises, can add Victorian romance, charm. The newer metal cake-forms made it possible to bake cakes in whimsical shapes such as fans, hearts, and rings.

Victorian-style cake with lacework, ribbon.

❧ *Bridal bouquet re-created as a sugar-paste delicacy.*

In most cultures, it's considered unlucky for a bride to bake her own wedding cake or taste even the frosting before she's officially wed. In early America, as in England, the traditional wedding cake was a dark fruitcake, often soaked in liquor, that could be easily stored and grew tastier with time. It was considered good luck and an omen for a long life together if the couple saved the top tier, or at least a piece—even a crumb—to eat on their first anniversary, or after the christening of their first child.

Decorated with charms, fleurs-de-lis, family names.

Today, in the southern United States, the baker places charms beneath the top tier as harbingers of the future. Before the cake cutting, each bridesmaid pulls a ribbon; attached may be a tiny ring ("next to marry"), heart ("love will come"), anchor ("hope, adventure"), thimble and button ("old maid"), horseshoe and four-leaf clover ("good luck"), or fleur-de-lis ("love will flower").

Centerpiece cake reminiscent of Wedgwood's blue Jasper.

Edible to the last sugar flower and bite of white wicker basket.

Stylish or fanciful, cake toppers today reflect the personal flair of the wedding couple. Whimsical ornaments (such as his-and-her jewel-studded riding boots) may commemorate how the bride and groom met, or where they're headed (two lovebirds perched atop the Eiffel Tower). Likenesses of the couple may be re-created with edible food color on a "canvas" of rolled marzipan; as photographic silhouettes, statuesque on the summit. Personalized sculptures of papier-mâché, brass, or ceramic incorporate hobbies (skiers poised to jump off the top tier) or careers (figures sitting on the scales of justice and a piano for the union of a lawyer and musician). Cake

cake toppers

[TOP] ❧ *Alluring antebellum romance: a cake with filigreed fan, cascading orchids.*
[BOTTOM] ❧ *A cake speaking the language of flowers: roses — love; sweet peas — voyage.*

toppers may also be commissioned sculptures: a hopeful frog-prince of blown glass or a sailing sloop in sterling silver. Some couples select a porcelain statue and then build their collection with each anniversary. Statuettes of the bridal couple, their cars and pets, may be cast in chocolate and marzipan, an echo of the molded-sugar creations of the sixteenth century. Antique cake toppers used at each family wedding whisper the hopes and dreams of yesteryear, continuing the ongoing life cycle. Another Victorian custom: topping a wedding cake with a nosegay of vibrant fresh blossoms (avoid poisonous flowers, such as lily of the valley) or the lush bounty of cascading fruit and nuts.

[TOP] ❧ *Fresh flowers adorn a garden-wedding cake.*
[BOTTOM] ❧ *Traditional bride-and-groom topper on a classic swagged cake.*

*the tradition of cutting
the cake*

The cake-cutting ceremony is usually just before dessert at a luncheon or dinner reception, or just after all the guests have been formally received at a cocktail or tea reception. To get everyone's attention, the band may play a fanfare to signal the moment, then direct the guests' attention to the wedding cake.

Some couples tie a festive ribbon around the cake knife from their newly selected sterling-silver pattern; others may use an heirloom knife (from their parents' wedding?). Some couples receive a keepsake called a "heritage knife" from their parents at the

A whimsical mini - wedding cake cookie.

time of the engagement. This new tradition symbolizes a celebration of common ancestry, yet recognizes each bride's uniqueness. The knife should be engraved on the spine with the couple's initials or joint monogram, perhaps their wedding date on back; it becomes a treasured serving piece to be used on family holidays and will be proudly passed on to following generations for additional engraving before each wedding.

Other creative ways to make the cut: Home renovators might use a shiny new saw; medical students might make the incision with a silver scalpel; gardeners, with a silver-plated trowel; and members of the military, with a saber, or sword.

According to tradition, the bride must cut the first piece or be childless and unhappy. To slice the cake, the groom places his right hand over the bride's while she holds the knife (this custom perhaps began as a symbol of the joy that was shared by the couple). Together they cut two small pieces from the back of the bottom tier (so the cake is still beautiful), then feed each other a bite (their first shared meal together). Be gentle when feeding your spouse; a wedding is no place for a food fight!

As a gracious gesture, the bride and groom might each serve pieces of wedding cake to their new in-laws. Then, the caterer should take over, wheeling the cake out of sight for cutting and serving. At royal weddings, it is customary for the first piece of the cake to be precut and the wedge iced back into place. Princess Elizabeth had no trouble cutting the first piece of cake at her wedding on November 20, 1947; she sliced over a precut area with Prince Philip's sword and then pulled a bowed ribbon to release the designated piece.

Sugar artistry: soft drapes and roses adorn each tier.

Display the wedding cake where it can be seen, but not damaged, on a separate cake table — out of the line of traffic. Outdoors, position cake in the shade on a sturdy stand or flat surface (especially if it's in a tent or on the grass). Surround a Victorian wedding cake

cake tables

(right) with bountiful bowls of fresh fruit, sumptuous floral arrangements. Drape the cake table in a cover matching the style, theme, season, of the wedding: a country quilt for a casual picnic, an antique lace cloth

⋙ Witty architectural confection with sugar topper.

for an afternoon cocktail reception, taffeta to coordinate with attendants' dresses. Accent table with strands of leaves, flowers, pine boughs, maids' bouquets; pin single blossoms, stems, in a cascade on a white cloth (left); link romantic garlands of greenery, diaphanous tulle, to cloth and chairs (left); sash airy trains of tulle to chair arms. To enhance the cake display, set out family photos. A satellite stand positions a large base cake with smaller cakes linked with ribbons, bridges, fountains, twinkling lights. A staircase staggers tiers in an oval around a fountain or rotating base.

Tulle, ribbon-and-leaf garlands, unify table, reception.

During the Middle Ages, printers used monograms as an identification shorthand. Emperors and kings marked coins, stationery, and possessions.

Every couple is royal on their wedding day. Print family seals or a joint monogram on thank-you notes, place cards, napkins, matchbooks, menu cards, favors, the cake boxes sent home with guests. Include initials on the cake in edible gold leaf or spun sugar. Personal insignias can also be embroidered on the bridal-table linen and on decorative reception-seat slipcovers.

Grace newlyweds' places of honor with handthreaded rose chains.

During the 1860s, the customary white wedding cake (often a rich pound cake) became known as the bride's cake, while the dark fruitcake was the groom's cake. It was the groom's cake that was boxed for single wedding guests to take home and slip under their pillow—to dream of their future mate. For single women, these "dream cakes" were wrapped with strips of paper bearing the names of unmarried men. Today the groom's cake may be the top layer of the wedding cake, and may be cut, boxed, or frozen for the first anniversary. Or, it might be served before the wedding—as the dessert at the rehearsal dinner or a surprise at the bachelor party.

groom's cake

The groom decides on the flavor, shape, and decorations. Many cakes are shapes symbolic of hobbies, pastimes, careers—a surfboard, golf course, sports car, gavel—or may be a family tradition (e.g., an armadillo cake).

To salute heritage, choose a shamrock cake laced with an Irish liqueur. Restoring a home? Design a gingerbread-house cake. To announce a surprise honeymoon destination: top a groom's cake with a miniature Acropolis.

Chocolate-mocha groom's (dream) cake boxed as guest favors.

one great cake recipe

[LEMON-MOUSSE WEDDING CAKE]

24 EGGS
3 CUPS SUGAR
6 CUPS CAKE FLOUR
1 CUP POPPY SEEDS (OPTIONAL)
9 TBS. GRATED LEMON RIND
8 TBS. MELTED BUTTER

Preheat oven to 350° F. Butter and flour two each: 6-inch, 10-inch, 14-inch cake pans, and line with parchment paper. Beat room-temperature eggs until light and creamy (volume should be about 4 times original). Add sugar. Sift flour into separate bowl, add poppy seeds (if desired), then fold into egg mixture. Mix in rind and butter. Fill pans 3/4 full and bake for 30 minutes or until toothpick inserted in center comes out clean. Cool on rack; remove from pans.

[LEMON-MOUSSE FILLING]

16 EGGS
3 CUPS SUGAR
12 TBS. LEMON JUICE
8 TSP. GRATED LEMON RIND

2 TSP. VANILLA
6 CUPS WHIPPING CREAM, WHIPPED
12 TBS. SUGAR

Use cake pans to trace 3 cardboard rounds (one of each size); set aside. Separate eggs; set aside egg whites. Mix together yolks, 3 cups sugar, lemon juice and lemon rind in top of double boiler. Place over simmering (not boiling) water. Stir constantly until thick. Remove from heat; cool in refrigerator until very cold. Add vanilla, whipped cream. Beat egg whites with remaining sugar until soft peaks form. Fold into custard and chill for 2 hours or until set. Level tops of cakes; slice each cake in half forming 4 equal layers. To assemble tiers: Spread a small amount of mousse (to anchor cake) on largest cardboard round; place first layer on top. On top of this cake, spread a 1/2-inch layer of mousse. Top with another round and 1/2-inch layer of mousse. Repeat until all cake layers of the same size are used. Top with next largest cardboard round and follow same procedure for remaining 2 cakes.

OPTIONS FOR ICING THE CAKE:
BUTTERCREAM, WHIPPED CREAM, ROLLED FONDANT
SERVES 125–150.

The term toasting wasn't used until the sixteenth century—when well-wishers placed a spicy crouton in the goblet, either for flavor or nourishment. The last to drink claimed the tasty morsel (the "toast") along with the good wishes. Today, the best man makes the first toast at the reception after all guests are through the receiving line and have a glass of champagne or any sparkling beverage.

toasting lore

A wedding toast should mention the occasion, the names of the couple being toasted, the speaker's relationship to the couple (e.g., how they met), and include good-luck sentiments for their future. It is customary for the groom to respond, thanking the best man, his parents and new in-laws. The bride may then wish to make her own toast, followed by the couple's parents, guests. Rise to give a toast and stay seated to receive one.

Art-deco cake in black, gold, silver, expresses style, enhances theme.

GROOM TO FRIENDS:

May the roof over us never fall in,
and may we friends gathered below never fall out.
—IRISH ANONYMOUS

However rare true love is, true friendship is rarer.
—FRANCOIS LA ROCHEFOUCAULD

sentimental toasts

Laugh and be merry together, like brothers akin,
Guesting awhile in the room of a beautiful inn.
Glad till the dancing stops, and the lilt of the music ends.
Laugh till the game is played; and be you merry my friends.
—JOHN MASEFIELD

TO THE BRIDE AND GROOM:

Look down you gods,
And on this couple drop a blessed crown.
—WILLIAM SHAKESPEARE

May your hands be forever clasped in friendship
and your hearts joined forever in love.

—ANONYMOUS

May the road rise to meet you.
May the wind be always at your back,
the sun shine warm upon your face,
the rain fall soft upon your fields,
and until we meet again
may God hold you in the hollow of His hand.

—IRISH BLESSING

PARENTS' TOASTS:

Here's to marriage, that happy estate that resembles a pair of
scissors. So joined that they cannot be separated, often moving in
opposite directions, yet punishing anyone who comes between them.

—SYDNEY SMITH

It is written: When children find true love,
parents find true joy.
Here's to your joy and ours, from this day forward.

—ANONYMOUS

one great punch recipe

[BRIDAL CHAMPAGNE PUNCH]

APPROXIMATELY 1 CUP SEASONAL FRUITS,
SUCH AS PEELED ORANGE SECTIONS,
SLICED LEMON, STAR FRUIT, PINEAPPLE,
STRAWBERRIES
6 OUNCES COGNAC (OR TO TASTE)
BLOCK OF ICE
1 BOTTLE CHILLED CHAMPAGNE
6 OUNCES SPARKLING WATER OR CLUB SODA
JUICE OF MARASCHINO CHERRIES TO TASTE FOR
SWEETNESS AND COLOR (OPTIONAL)

When ready to serve, place the fruits of your choice in a large punch bowl and add the cognac. Add the block of ice and pour the champagne and sparkling water over it. Stir briefly, taking care not to flatten the bubbles. If desired, add a tiny bit of maraschino-cherry juice and stir gently again. Serve in chilled wineglass or punch cup.

MAKES APPROXIMATELY NINE FOUR-OUNCE SERVINGS.